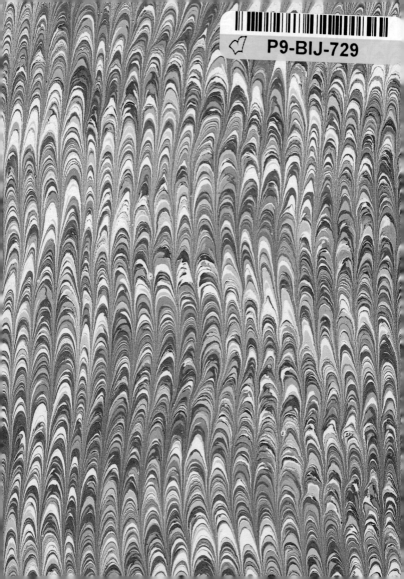

P9-BIJ-729

THE BANTAM LIBRARY
of Culinary Arts

GARLIC
& Onions

JILL NORMAN

BANTAM BOOKS
NEW YORK · TORONTO · LONDON · SYDNEY · AUCKLAND

A DORLING KINDERSLEY BOOK

GARLIC & ONIONS
A BANTAM BOOK/PUBLISHED BY ARRANGEMENT WITH
DORLING KINDERSLEY LIMITED

PRINTING HISTORY
DORLING KINDERSLEY EDITION
PUBLISHED IN GREAT BRITAIN IN 1992

BANTAM EDITION/MAY 1992

EDITOR   MARK RONAN
SENIOR EDITOR   CAROLYN RYDEN
AMERICAN EDITOR   BECKY CABAZA
DESIGN   MATHEWSON BULL
PHOTOGRAPHER   DAVE KING

Every effort has been made to provide accurate conversions from metric to American measures,
though some ingredient amounts have been rounded off to the closest American measure.

LIBRARY OF CONGRESS CATALOGING-IN-PUBLICATION DATA
NORMAN, JILL.
GARLIC & ONIONS/JILL NORMAN.
P. CM. — (BANTAM LIBRARY OF CULINARY ARTS)
INCLUDES INDEX.
ISBN 0–553–08293–0
1. COOKERY (GARLIC) 2. COOKERY (ONIONS) 3. GARLIC. 4. ONIONS.
I. TITLE. II. TITLE: GARLIC AND ONIONS.
TX819.G3N67 1992
641.6′526—DC20
91-33105 CIP

BANTAM BOOKS ARE PUBLISHED BY BANTAM BOOKS, A DIVISION OF BANTAM
DOUBLEDAY DELL PUBLISHING GROUP, INC. ITS TRADEMARK, CONSISTING OF THE
WORDS "BANTAM BOOKS" AND THE PORTRAYAL OF A ROOSTER, IS REGISTERED IN
U.S. PATENT AND TRADEMARK OFFICE AND IN OTHER COUNTRIES, MARCA
REGISTRADA. BANTAM BOOKS, 666 FIFTH AVENUE, NEW YORK, NEW YORK 10103

PRINTED AND BOUND IN HONG KONG BY IMAGO
0 9 8 7 6 5 4 3 2 1

C O N T E N T S

INTRODUCTION

*T*HERE are some 500 members of the Alliaceae, or onion family. Most of them are edible, but not necessarily good to eat. Many still grow wild, others – garlic, leeks, onions – have been cultivated for thousands of years. The Hebrews fleeing Egypt bewailed their lost foods: "We remember the fish, which we did eat in Egypt freely; the cucumbers and the melons, and the leeks, and the onions and the garlick." Numbers XI, 5.

Garlic plant

Today the onion family still provides the most popular flavoring vegetables; both onions and garlic come into the top 20 vegetables grown worldwide. Different regions and countries all have their own preferences; in recent times Western cooks have learned from the Japanese and Chinese about wider uses for green onions and some of their varieties are now being cultivated in Europe and North America. Leeks and shallots often seem to be underrated, but Asian cooks may again provide inspiration, for leeks are a favorite vegetable in northern China, and shallots are prized for their subtle flavors in the south. In the Middle East onions are often put into a dish at the beginning of the cooking time to impart a mellow flavor, then one or two more are added near the end to give more piquancy and texture.

No other vegetable arouses as many passions as garlic. History and literature record that dislike of garlic was not limited to the northern regions of the world, although it is usually the timid northerner who is depicted as fearing garlic. And until recently the garlic-lover faced deprivation in parts of Britain and North America. Digestive problems usually arise, not from the amount of garlic eaten, but from eating the central green shoot. Garlic, however, is usually disliked for its odor on the breath, which derives from the sulphur compounds present in the plant oils which are excreted via the lungs. Cooked garlic has a much less pronounced smell than raw. An agriculturalist from Japan has produced a processed form of garlic which is said to be odorless – not garlic without an aroma, but garlic that doesn't taint the breath. Not yet marketed in any significant quantity, it still remains to be seen whether the claims made for odorless garlic are true. In European cooking there used to be

Garlic seller from
Normandy

a clear distinction, now somewhat blurred, between southern garlic- and oil-based cuisines and those of the north which used onions or shallots and butter. The great chef, Marcel Boulestin, maintained that peace and happiness begin where garlic is used in cooking.

GARLIC

*G*ARLIC, Allium sativum, *is native to the steppes of central Asia, but soon found its way to the Middle East, where it was popular with the Babylonians, the Hebrews and the Egyptians. The pyramid at Giza had an inscription telling how much garlic and onion had been consumed by the men who built it and Olympic athletes were said to eat large quantities of garlic to build up their strength.*

Homer, Aristotle, Virgil, Pliny and Mohammed all enthused about the properties of this pungent and versatile plant, in those times used for medicine and magic rather than as food. The Greeks placed it at crossroads for Hecate, goddess of the underworld. Travelers carried it to protect them from her.

It was widely believed that garlic could ward off evil, whether evil spirits, witches, demons or vampires. Pliny recorded that its smell would drive away snakes and scorpions; Mohammed that garlic applied to stings or bites

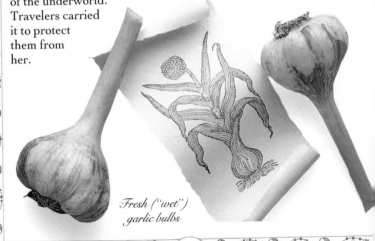

Fresh ("wet") garlic bulbs

of poisonous animals would bring relief to the victim. The herbalists of the 16th and 17th centuries noted the same virtues, and Parkinson also advocated garlic as an antidote to drinking poison such as hemlock or wolfsbane (*Theatrum Botanicum*, 1640). Garlic might be rubbed on a wound, infused or boiled, but the herbalists frequently noted that it was not eaten raw: the odor was too powerful. They also recommended various breath fresheners after eating garlic, including the bitter herb, rue, roasted beets and parsley – a remedy still suggested today. In contemporary medicine garlic is regarded as a powerful healing plant. It is thought to be effective against cancer, lung and digestive infections, arthritis and rheumatism, but is best known for protecting the cardiovascular system, lowering blood pressure and cholesterol. It is antifungal, antibacterial and antiviral, and has virtually no side-effects.

String of garlic

CULTIVATION &
VARIETIES

*G*ARLIC GROWS BEST *in a rich, moist soil; in heavy clay dig in some sand before planting. A sunny position is best. Although garlic certainly has a stronger flavor when grown in a warm climate, it is hardy enough for cooler regions, where it tends to do better with a longer growing season. Break a head of garlic into cloves and plant them 2 in/5 cm deep and 5 in/12 cm apart. The freshly harvested "wet" garlic is succulent and mild; if the heads are hung up to dry the flavor will intensify.*

In Spain fresh garlic shoots are a delicacy fried for *tapas*. Mild "wet" garlic (see p. 6), with its thick green stalk and large juicy cloves, is excellent for lightly flavoring summer vegetables and salads.

Pink garlic (**ail rose**) *head and clove*

Garlic may have a white, violet or pink skin, depending on the variety. Pink garlic, *ail rose*, from Lautrec in southwest France has an appellation guaranteeing its provenance and quality, indicated on its red label.

Large garlic head

White-skinned garlic heads and cloves

Pink-skinned garlic heads

GARLIC IN THE KITCHEN

*G*OOD GARLIC IS FIRM, *with no brown spots, and the cloves have not shrivelled in the papery skin. Store in a cool, dry place, preferably where the air can circulate around the heads. Whole garlic has no smell; when it is crushed or chopped, a sulphur compound is released which oxidizes in contact with air, producing the characteristic garlic odor. Whole cloves cooked slowly have a mellow, nutty taste; that of cut garlic is more pungent, even when cooked.*

Chopped garlic

Crush garlic by putting an unpeeled clove under a large, flat knife-blade and pressing down on it. The skin will come loose. It is easily pounded in a mortar with the addition of a little salt. A garlic press adds a crude metallic taste to the crushed garlic and is best avoided. A light flavor of raw garlic can be added to a dish by using garlic oil or vinegar or serving with garlic butter. A whole clove gently sautéed in oil and removed before other ingredients are added will give a delicate flavor; a crushed clove rather more. Do not let garlic burn or it develops a bitter, acrid taste.

Crushed cloves   *Pounded garlic*

ONIONS: THEIR HISTORY & CULTIVATION

*O*NIONS, Allium cepa, *have been cultivated around the world for thousands of years, and their origin is obscure. Like garlic, they have an enviable record as a health-giving food. In* Paradisi in Sole, *1656, Parkinson noted that onion juice was beneficial for burns or scalds and that boiled or roasted onion mixed with sugar and butter would help clear a cough. Today the onion's ability to combat colds and infections is widely recognized, and medical research shows that it is helpful in lowering blood sugar, reducing cholesterol and eliminating fatty deposits.*

Spanish onion vendor

Onion seeds

Onions are easy to grow, provided the bed is deeply dug and well manured. Seeds planted in late summer will yield a crop the following summer; seeds or sets (immature bulbs) planted in spring can be harvested in the autumn. When the tops begin to yellow bend them down to encourage ripening. Lift the onions and spread out to dry completely before stringing them or putting them in a net to hang for winter storage. Onions that have sprouted, feel soft or smell musty should be avoided; they invariably have a poor flavor.

ONION VARIETIES

*T*HERE ARE ABOUT *500 varieties of culti-vated and wild onions, with different colors, textures and tastes. They are in greater demand in the kitchen than any other vegetable. Onions vary in quality and intensity of flavor depending on the level of sulphurous constituents in the volatile oil. As with garlic, these are responsible for the aroma and taste, which may be sweet or sharp. Compounds released when an onion is cut make the eyes water and smart.*

Red onions may be sweet or sharp, but those commercially available tend to be mild, suitable for eating raw.

Red onions

"Spanish" onion

Large brown-skinned "Spanish" onions have a mild flavor. They are good baked or used in marinades for raw fish.

Small brown- and yellow-skinned onions are essential to the cook as an all-purpose flavoring.

White onions have a sharp flavor. They can be used for preparing dishes that look more attractive with whole, small onions.

Small brown-skinned onion

White onions

MORE VARIETIES

GREEN ONIONS ARE *the largest onion crop grown in China and Japan. The Japanese have developed many varieties, with and without bulbs, all with long-lasting green tops. They have a mild flavor and both the white stem and leaves may be eaten. Oriental varieties are sometimes available from oriental supermarkets, but scallions may be used instead.*

Cocktail onions are usually prepared with mild, white silverskins. They are sown deep to prevent them turning green. Seldom offered for sale fresh, most go for processing.

Japanese bunching, or welsh onions, are a variety of *Allium fistulosum*, and widely grown in the Far East. Oriental cooks use them as an ingredient and a garnish; they are excellent chopped into a clear soup. Scallions are seed onions harvested when green and young. They are grown from different varieties; if the green leaves are round and hollow they are welsh onions; if flattened, a Western variety.

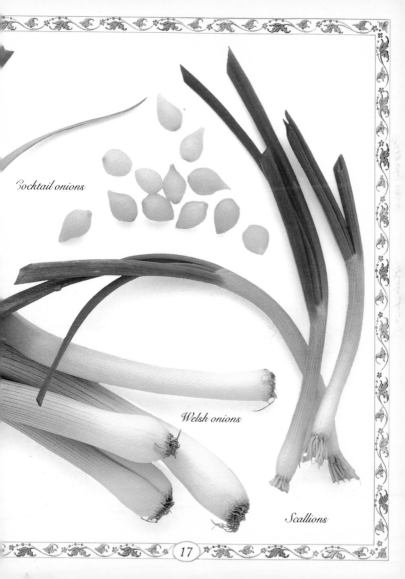

Cocktail onions

Welsh onions

Scallions

SHALLOTS

*E*ASILY GROWN IN *a sunny spot that has previously been well manured for another crop, shallots are a frost-hardy variety of onion, and can be planted in winter or early spring. Push the bulb into the ground but leave the tip protruding. When the foliage dies back in summer, harvest the shallots, leave to dry, then store in a net in a cool, dry place. Shallots form a cluster of bulbs instead of a single one like other onions. They are round or elongated, red, golden brown or grey-skinned, depending on the variety.*

Red shallots

Long brown shallots

Brown shallots

Shallots have a more subtle flavor than onions and their smell is less overpowering. They vary in flavor according to the variety, soil and climate conditions. They are much used in French cooking, particularly in the north and Bordeaux. In Western cooking shallots are used raw in salads; braised whole in stews and casseroles; cooked slowly in fat or boiled down with wine before being added to a dish. In Southeast Asia they are pounded with galangal, lemon grass and chilies to make a fragrant seasoning, or sliced and fried for a crisp garnish.

LEEKS

*L*EEKS, Allium porrum, the mildest of the onion family, have been cultivated for thousands of years. They are easy to grow, but need a long growing season. Seeds are sown in spring and the young leeks planted out in summer. During autumn the soil must be drawn around the base of the plants to blanch them. They can be left in the ground through the winter and picked as needed.

Leeks

Leeks are an important flavoring in many meat and vegetable soups and stews. A good addition to a bouquet garni, leeks also marry well with olives and with aniseed flavors. Young leeks can be used raw in salads.

CHIVES

*T*HE SMALLEST MEMBER *of the onion family,* Allium
schoenoprasum, *grows easily in a pot or in the kitchen gar-
den. The tubular grass-like stalks can be chopped finely for soups,
sauces, salads and other dishes, or tied ele-
gantly around small bundles of julienned
vegetables. The mauve flowers look attractive
in green salads. The flavor of chives is defi-
nitely onion, but it is light and subtle with
spicy overtones.*

Chives

Garlic chives, *A. tuberosum,* have flat leaves and
white flowers. The tighter the bud, the better the
quality; those with open flowers are
considered too old to eat.

While chives taste of onion, garlic chives taste of
garlic and need to be chopped finely if used raw
because of their tough texture. In China they may
be served cooked as a vegetable.

Garlic chives

Recipes

*All the recipes are for 4,
but some may serve more*

Spanish Garlic Soup

A wonderful soup for a raw winter day, and very easy to prepare.

4 tablespoons olive oil
4 cloves garlic, crushed
4 slices stale bread
1 teaspoon paprika
4 cups/900 ml water
salt
4 eggs

Heat the oil in a heavy pan and fry the garlic and slices of bread slowly until golden. Remove them from the pan and stir in the paprika. Pour in the water, add salt and return the garlic to the soup. Bring to the boil, then simmer for 10 minutes. Break the eggs into small bowls and slide them into the soup to poach for 4–5 minutes. Put the slices of bread on top of the soup, and serve.

FRENCH GARLIC SOUP

4 cups/1 liter water
5 cloves garlic, crushed
1 egg, separated
salt and pepper
3 oz/75 g vermicelli
½ teaspoon mustard
¼ cup/75 ml olive oil

Bring the water to the boil in a large pan and add the garlic and egg white. Season with salt and pepper, stir well and simmer for 5 minutes. Boil the vermicelli in a separate pan until al dente, then drain. Beat the egg yolk with the mustard and a little salt and pepper, then add the oil, a little at a time, beating as you do so, to make a mayonnaise. Stir a ladleful of warm soup into the mayonnaise, then pour the mixture back into the soup, add the vermicelli, remove from the heat and serve.

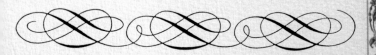

GARLIC PURÉE

This purée, which is not overpowering, can be used to flavor soups, sauces and vegetable purées. It is good with roast lamb too.

10 heads young garlic
salt
2 tablespoons olive oil

Use unblemished, firm heads of garlic and avoid any that have a green shoot in the center. Put the whole heads in a pan and cover with boiling water. Simmer for 15–20 minutes, until the flesh is very soft. Drain and allow to cool, then remove the skins and blend in a processor or push through a fine sieve. Season the purée with a little salt and stir in the oil. The purée will keep for a week or two in the refrigerator if stored in a jar, covered with more olive oil.

Muhamara

4 oz/125 g walnuts
2 cloves garlic, crushed
3 tablespoons fresh breadcrumbs
1 tablespoon tomato purée
2 tablespoons chopped parsley
2 tablespoons lemon juice
salt
3 tablespoons olive oil
1 teaspoon paprika

Pound the walnuts to a paste, then add all the other ingredients, or put everything into a food processor and blend to a coarse paste. Serve with a little olive oil dribbled over the top and a sprinkling of paprika.

Stir-Fried Spinach with Garlic

A simple dish that is good served hot or cold.

2 lb/1 kg spinach
1 tablespoon oil
3 cloves garlic, crushed
$^1/_2$ teaspoon salt
$^1/_2$ teaspoon sugar

Wash the spinach and drain well. Remove any tough stalks and cut the spinach into wide ribbons. Heat a wok or frying pan, add the oil, swirl it around to coat the pan, and put in the garlic. Fry for a few seconds, then add the spinach and salt. Toss and fry for 1 minute, and put in the sugar. Stir-fry for 2 minutes more, then remove from the pan. Do not cook longer or the spinach may get watery.

GARLIC POTATOES

1½ lb/750 g new potatoes
3 tablespoons olive oil
12 large cloves garlic, peeled

Scrub the potatoes and put them in a shallow oiled earthenware casserole. Put the whole garlic cloves among them and pour over the rest of the oil, making sure all the vegetables are well coated. Add 6 tablespoons of water, cover the casserole and bake in a preheated oven, 450°F/230°C, for 20 minutes. Then turn the potatoes and return the dish, uncovered, to the oven for a further 25–30 minutes, until the potatoes are cooked and their skins lightly browned.

POACHED COD WITH AIOLI

a cod weighing 3–4 lb/1.5–2 kg
4–6 cloves garlic
salt
2 egg yolks
1¼ cups/300 ml olive oil
juice of 1 lemon

Put the cod in a fish kettle or large pan, cover with water, put a lid on the pan and bring slowly to the boil. Let the water bubble for a minute, then remove the pan from the heat and leave until the water is cold. The fish will be perfectly cooked.

To make the aioli pound the garlic and a little salt to a paste in a mortar. Add the egg yolks and beat until pale or combine the garlic and yolks in a processor. Pour in the oil in a thin thread, beating as you do so. After adding 3–4 tablespoons of the oil beat in a teaspoon of warm water. Continue adding the oil and beating well until the aioli thickens. When most of the oil has been used, add the lemon juice and another teaspoon of warm water. Finish up the oil; by this time the aioli should be very thick and smooth.

Drain the cod, remove the skin and place on a serving dish. Serve with the aioli and boiled new potatoes.

RABBIT WITH GARLIC

1 rabbit, cut up
salt and pepper
²/₃ cup/150 ml olive oil
40 cloves garlic, unpeeled
large bouquet of herbs – thyme,
parsley, bay leaves, celery,
marjoram

Season the rabbit with salt and
pepper and put it into an
earthenware casserole with the
oil and garlic. Mix well to ensure
that everything is evenly coated
with oil. Bury the bouquet in the
middle. Put a double layer of foil
over the casserole, and then
cover with its lid. Bake in a
preheated oven, 375°F/
190°C, for 1½ hours. Serve with
slices of lightly toasted bread on
which the garlic can be spread.

CHICKEN WITH GARLIC AND LEMON

1 chicken, cut in serving pieces
salt and pepper
olive oil
1 medium onion, sliced
12 cloves garlic, peeled
3 oz/75 g serrano ham, cut in strips
2 lemons
4 tablespoons amontillado sherry
1¼ cups/300 ml chicken stock

Rub the chicken pieces with salt
and pepper and sauté in the olive
oil until lightly browned on all
sides. Remove them from the
pan and cook the onion gently
until soft and golden. Add the
whole garlic cloves and the ham
and cook for a further 6–8
minutes, stirring frequently,
until all is well blended.
Remove the zest from the
lemons, then take off and
discard the pith, and cut the
lemons into thin slices. Return
the chicken to the pan with the
lemon zest and slices, the sherry
and the stock.
Bring gently to the boil, then
reduce the heat, and simmer,
covered, for about 50 minutes,
until the chicken is tender. Lift
the pieces out onto a serving
dish. If necessary, boil down the
liquid for a few minutes to
reduce it somewhat, then spoon
it over and around the chicken
and serve.

CHICKEN TABAKA

A celebrated garlic-lovers' dish from Soviet Georgia.

1 medium chicken
salt
red pepper
10 cloves garlic
3 tablespoons/50 g butter
2 tablespoons oil
²/₃ cup/150 ml stock or water
2 scallions, chopped
1 tablespoon chopped parsley

Cut the chicken lengthwise along the breastbone and take out the bone, so that the bird will lie flat. Beat to flatten further. Make small slits in the skin to tuck the ends of the legs and wings into. Rub the chicken all over with salt and red pepper and one crushed clove of garlic. Refrigerate for a few hours, if possible, for the flavors to develop. Heat the butter and oil in a heavy frying pan, put in the chicken, skin side down, and put a weight on top: use a tin plate or another pan with a weight of 5–10 lb/2.5–5 kg resting on it. Fry the chicken over low to medium heat for 20–30 minutes, until it is golden brown. Make sure it doesn't burn. Turn it over, put back the weight and fry on the other side, again for 20–30 minutes.

While the chicken is cooking, prepare the sauce. Pound the rest of the garlic to a paste with a little salt, then pour on the boiling stock or water. Stir in the scallions and parsley and serve with the chicken.

CHILBUR

A Turkish dish of poached eggs
and stewed onions from
A Manual of Turkish Cookery by
Turabi Efendi, 1862.

"Peel and slice fine *three or four onions*, and fry them a nice brown in fresh *butter*, lay them on the bottom of a dish, and keep it hot; then pour in a pan *a pint of water*, add a little *salt*, and *a tablespoonful of vinegar*, put it on the fire, when boiling, break carefully in the pan *six or seven eggs*, simmer till the white is firm, then take them out with a slice, and arrange them over the onions; then pour a little hot fresh butter over them, sprinkle a little *pepper* and powdered *cinnamon* over, and serve hot."

DUTCH ONION PANCAKES

4 cups/1 liter milk
¹⁄₂ oz/15 g dried yeast
1 lb/500 g flour
salt and pepper
3 eggs, beaten
4 tablespoons/75 g butter
1¹⁄₂ lb/750 g onions, thinly sliced

Heat the milk to lukewarm and prove the yeast in a little of it. Sift the flour into a mixing bowl, add salt and pepper, make a well in the center and pour in the yeast and eggs. Draw in the flour and add the remaining milk, a little at a time, stirring to make a smooth batter. Cover and put aside to rise for an hour or so.

Melt 3 tablespoons/50 g of the butter in a heavy pan and stew the onions gently until they are soft and golden. Add them to the batter and leave to rise for a further 30 minutes.

Melt a very small amount of butter in a frying pan, just enough to grease the bottom, and pour in a ladleful of batter. Fry each pancake until lightly browned on both sides.

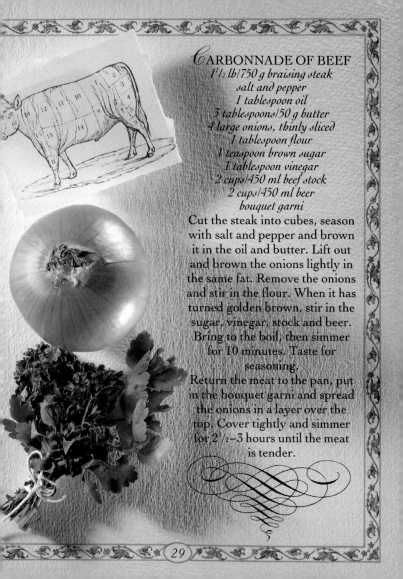

CARBONNADE OF BEEF

1½ lb/750 g braising steak
salt and pepper
1 tablespoon oil
3 tablespoons/50 g butter
4 large onions, thinly sliced
1 tablespoon flour
1 teaspoon brown sugar
1 tablespoon vinegar
2 cups/450 ml beef stock
2 cups/450 ml beer
bouquet garni

Cut the steak into cubes, season
with salt and pepper and brown
it in the oil and butter. Lift out
and brown the onions lightly in
the same fat. Remove the onions
and stir in the flour. When it has
turned golden brown, stir in the
sugar, vinegar, stock and beer.
Bring to the boil, then simmer
for 10 minutes. Taste for
seasoning.
Return the meat to the pan, put
in the bouquet garni and spread
the onions in a layer over the
top. Cover tightly and simmer
for 2½–3 hours until the meat
is tender.

Oriental Onions

This is a French dish, in spite of its name.

2 lb/1 kg small white or pickling onions
3 tomatoes, peeled, seeded and chopped
1¼ cups/300 ml dry white wine
⅔ cup/150 ml olive oil
1 teaspoon coriander seeds
½ teaspoon paprika
salt and pepper

Put the peeled onions in a pan that will hold them in one layer. Add the tomato pulp and pour over the wine and oil – there should be enough just to cover the onions. Season with coriander, paprika, salt and pepper. Cover and bring to the boil. Simmer for about 20 minutes, until the onions are cooked. Turn into a bowl and leave to cool.

Baked Onions

Cut *4 large onions* in half horizontally and put them in a baking dish just big enough to hold them tightly. Sprinkle over *1 tablespoon crumbled rosemary* and *1 tablespoon brown sugar* and season with *salt and pepper*. Pour on *3 tablespoons each of wine vinegar and olive oil* and *6 tablespoons water*, then bake in a preheated oven, 400°F/200°C, for 1 hour, basting frequently. The liquid should be absorbed when the onions are cooked.

Onions in Cream

2 lb/1 kg onions
1/4 teaspoon mace
salt and pepper
3 tablespoons heavy cream
1 1/2 tablespoons/25 g butter

Peel the onions and blanch,
whole, in boiling salted water for
3–4 minutes. Drain thoroughly
and chop coarsely. Season with
mace, salt and plenty of black
pepper. Stir in the cream. Turn
the onions into a buttered
baking dish and dot the top with
the remaining butter. Bake in a
preheated oven, 375°F/190°C,
for 25–30 minutes.

Mexican Pickled Onions

A recipe from the Yucatán
peninsula in southern Mexico
where they are served with
panuchos, tortillas stuffed with
beans and chicken. They are
good with plain roast chicken
and with ham too.

1 lb/500 g red onions
salt
2 teaspoons crumbled oregano
1/2 teaspoon ground allspice
1/2 teaspoon ground cumin
1/2 teaspoon coarsely ground black
pepper
6 cloves garlic, sliced
1 1/4 cups/300 ml wine or cider vinegar

Slice the onions thinly and
blanch them in boiling salted
water for 1 minute. Combine the
herbs and spices and mix with
the onion and garlic in a glass or
china bowl. Pour over the
vinegar. Make sure there is
enough to cover the onions.
Leave to stand for several hours
before serving. The pickle will
improve over a few days, and
will keep for 2–3 weeks
in a jar in the
refrigerator.

ORIENTAL EGGPLANT SALAD

2 medium eggplants
2 tablespoons sesame oil
1 tablespoon fish sauce*
1 tablespoon light soy sauce
1 clove garlic, chopped finely
4 scallions, chopped finely
salt
cayenne

Prick the eggplants a few times
with a fork and bake in a
preheated oven, 350°F/
180°C, for about 20 minutes,
until soft. When cool, cut off the
stalks and peel. Squeeze out any
excess liquid and chop the flesh
roughly. Combine the sesame
oil, fish sauce and soy with the
garlic and scallion. Taste and
add salt if necessary.
Put the eggplant in a shallow
dish, spoon over the dressing
and dust with cayenne.

° Fish sauce is a clear
brown liquid drained off
fish that has been
fermented in brine. It is
available from oriental
shops.

ONION AND ORANGE SALAD

4 large oranges
1 red onion, thinly sliced
a few small black olives
3 tablespoons olive oil
1 tablespoon lemon juice
1/2 teaspoon paprika
salt

Remove all the peel and pith from the oranges and slice them into a shallow bowl, keeping as much of the juice as possible. Arrange the onion slices and olives on top. Make a dressing with the oil, lemon juice, paprika and salt and pour over the salad.

COLD YOGURT SOUP

A refreshing summer soup.

2 cups/450 ml yogurt
1 1/4 cups/300 ml cold water
1 cucumber
4 scallions, chopped
3 tablespoons chopped dill
3 tablespoons chopped parsley
3 tablespoons chopped chives
salt and pepper

Stir the yogurt until smooth, then add the water. Peel the cucumber, remove the seeds and grate or chop the flesh finely. Add the cucumber, scallions and herbs to the yogurt; season and chill before serving.

SHALLOT SAUCE

To make a good simple sauce for grilled fish or steaks, chop 3 shallots finely and simmer in 2 tablespoons vinegar for 5 minutes, watching that the pan does not become dry. Add 4 tablespoons dry white wine, 1 tablespoon chopped parsley, a pat of butter and season with salt and pepper. Simmer for 5–10 minutes, then whisk in 3 tablespoons/50 g butter, a little at a time. Serve as soon as the butter is incorporated.

CÈPES À LA BORDELAISE

If you don't have cèpes you can make the dish with cultivated mushrooms, preferably the large flat ones.

1 lb/500 g cèpes
3 tablespoons/50 g butter
juice of 1/2 lemon
3 tablespoons olive oil
salt and pepper
3 shallots, chopped
3 tablespoons breadcrumbs
2 tablespoons chopped parsley

Remove the stalks from the mushrooms, trim them and cut in quarters, lengthwise. Put half the butter and the lemon juice into a pan, add the caps and stalks and stew gently until all the liquid has evaporated. Remove the cèpes from the pan and slice the caps. Heat the remaining butter with the oil, put back the caps and most of the stalks. Season with salt and pepper and sauté until lightly browned. Chop the remaining stalks finely. Just before serving add the chopped stalks, shallots, breadcrumbs and parsley to the pan. Stir through and serve.

SCALLOPS WITH RADICCHIO

1 head radicchio, shredded
3 tablespoons/50 g butter
12 scallops
1 tablespoon olive oil
3 shallots, chopped finely
1/2 glass dry white wine
salt and pepper
5 tablespoons heavy cream
breadcrumbs

Make a bed of radicchio in a buttered gratin dish. Cut the scallops in half horizontally. Heat 1 1/2 tablespoons/25 g butter and the oil in a small pan and stew the shallots gently for a few minutes. Add the wine and the scallops and cook for about a minute, until the scallops are opaque. Lift them out, drain and place on the radicchio. Reduce the cooking liquid to 3–4 tablespoons, season with salt and pepper and add the cream. Cook until the sauce thickens slightly, then spoon over the scallops and radicchio. Sprinkle breadcrumbs over the top, dot with a little butter and put under a hot grill for a few minutes to brown the top.

♪ PICED MONKFISH

2 lb/1 kg monkfish on the bone
1 stalk lemon grass, crushed
4 shallots, sliced
2 large cloves garlic, sliced
2 in/5 cm fresh ginger, sliced
¼ teaspoon chili powder
½ teaspoon ground cumin
½ teaspoon ground coriander
½ teaspoon turmeric
salt
1½ oz/40 g coconut cream*
¾ cup/175 ml hot water

Take an ovenproof dish into
which the monkfish will just fit
and put the lemon grass and half
the shallots, garlic and ginger on
the bottom. Rub the fish on both
sides with the mixed spices and a
little salt and lay it in the dish.
Put the remaining shallots,
garlic and ginger on top of the
fish. Mix the coconut cream
with the water and pour it over
the fish. Cover and bake in a
preheated oven, 350°F/
180°C, for 40 minutes. Serve
with rice garnished with lots of
green coriander.

* Coconut cream is a firm white block
of coconut paste which will keep
indefinitely. It can be bought from
oriental shops.

CHINESE BRAISED COD WITH SHALLOTS

4 cod steaks
salt
4 tablespoons oil
8 oz/250 g shallots, whole
a small piece of ginger, chopped finely
1 red chili
3 tablespoons light soy sauce
3 tablespoons dry sherry
1 tablespoon red wine vinegar
1 teaspoon sugar
2/3 cup/150 ml fish stock or water

Rub the steaks on both sides with salt. Heat the oil in a frying pan or wok and lightly brown the fish on both sides. Remove from the pan, drain off excess oil and add the shallots. Toss and fry for a minute or two, then add the ginger and chili. Stir-fry for a minute more, then add the rest of the ingredients. Bring to a simmer, put the fish steaks back in the pan and cook for 8–10 minutes until they are ready. Discard the chili and serve.

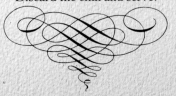

LEEK AND MUSSEL SOUP

2 lb/1 kg mussels
4 leeks, sliced
1 onion, chopped
2 stalks celery, chopped
1 carrot, sliced
2 cloves garlic, chopped
3 tablespoons/50 g butter
6 oz/175 g potatoes, diced
3 cups/750 ml water
salt and pepper
1 1/4 cups/300 ml cream or half-and-half
juice of 1/2 lemon

Clean the mussels, discarding any that are open or broken, and steam them open in a covered pan over high heat. Remove the mussels from their shells and strain the resulting liquid through muslin. Put both aside. Stew the leeks, onion, celery, carrot and garlic in the butter until soft, then add the potatoes and water, season with salt and pepper and simmer until the potatoes are soft. Purée the soup and stir in the cream and the mussels and their liquid. Heat gently, stir in the lemon juice and serve.

LEEK AND HAM QUICHE

1¼ cups/175 g flour
a pinch of salt
⅔ cup/150 g butter
a little water
2 lb/1 kg leeks
4 oz/125 g serrano ham
3 egg yolks
1¼ cups/300 ml light cream
a pinch of mace
salt and pepper

Make a shortcrust pastry: sift the flour with the salt, cut half the butter into small pieces and rub into the flour until it resembles fine breadcrumbs. Mix in just enough chilled water to bind the dough. Leave it to rest while you prepare the filling.

Cut the white part of the leeks in thin rounds and cook gently in most of the remaining butter until soft. Cut the serrano ham into small pieces and add to the pan. Cook a few minutes more. Roll out the pastry and line a 9 in/23 cm tart pan. Arrange the leeks and ham on the pastry. Beat the egg yolks, cream and seasonings together and pour over. Dot the top with the remaining butter. Bake in a preheated oven, 400°F/200°C, for 25–30 minutes, until puffed and brown.

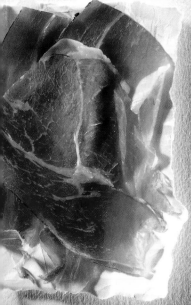

LEEKS IN RED WINE

2 lb/1 kg leeks
3 tablespoons/50 g butter
2 shallots, chopped
4 cloves garlic, peeled
bay leaf
a sprig of thyme
salt and pepper
²⁄₃ cup/150 ml red wine

Trim the tops from the leeks, but leave some of the green part. Blanch them in a pan of boiling salted water for 3–4 minutes, then drain thoroughly. Melt half the butter in a shallow ovenproof dish that will hold the leeks in a single layer and cook the shallots briefly. Put the leeks on top of the shallots, add the garlic and herbs. Season with salt and pepper. Pour over the wine. Cover and bake in a preheated oven, 350°F/180°C, for about 45 minutes. Transfer the leeks to a serving dish and keep warm. Discard the bay leaf and thyme. Boil the cooking liquid to reduce slightly and finish by whisking in the remaining butter, a little at a time. Pour the sauce over the leeks and serve.

LEEKS WITH CHICKPEAS AND TOMATOES

2 tablespoons olive oil
2 cloves garlic, chopped
6 scallions, chopped
6 tomatoes, peeled, seeded and chopped
1¹⁄₂ lb/750 g leeks
¹⁄₂ teaspoon paprika
salt and pepper
6 oz/175 g cooked chickpeas

Heat the oil in a pan and add the garlic and scallion. Fry gently for a few minutes then add the tomato. Cut the leeks into chunks and add them when the tomato and scallion have thickened to a sauce-like consistency. Pour in enough water just to cover the leeks, season with paprika, salt and pepper and simmer for 20 minutes. Stir in the chickpeas, being careful not to break up the leeks, and cook for a further 10 minutes or so, until the chickpeas are heated through.

Marinated Leeks

2 lb/1 kg young leeks
4 tablespoons olive oil
juice of 2 lemons
3 cloves garlic, lightly crushed
a sprig of thyme
salt and pepper
²/₃ cup/150 ml dry white wine
chopped parsley

Slice the leeks thickly. Put all the ingredients except the parsley into a pan and add boiling water just to cover the leeks. Simmer until the leeks are tender, 10–12 minutes. Turn into a bowl, sprinkle over the parsley and leave to cool.

Cucumber, Carrot and Radish Salad

1 cucumber
2 carrots
1 white radish (daikon)
3 tablespoons chives, chopped
1 tablespoon sesame oil
1 tablespoon rice or wine vinegar
1 tablespoon light soy sauce
1 teaspoon sugar
salt
cayenne

Cut the cucumber in half lengthwise, remove the seeds and cut it into thin strips. Cut the carrot and radish into similar matchstick pieces. Put the vegetables in a bowl and scatter over the chives. Make a dressing with the remaining ingredients, pour over the salad and leave to absorb the flavors for half an hour or so before serving.

ACKNOWLEDGMENTS

The publishers would like to thank the following:

JACKET
· PHOTOGRAPHY ·
DAVE KING

· TYPESETTING ·
TRADESPOOLS LTD
FROME

· ILLUSTRATOR ·
JANE THOMSON

PHOTOGRAPHIC
· ASSISTANCE ·
JONATHAN BUCKLEY

· REPRODUCTION ·
COLOURSCAN
SINGAPORE

PAGE 5 MARY EVANS PICTURE LIBRARY, LONDON
PAGE 12 THE MANSELL COLLECTION

CYNTHIA HOLE FOR PICTURE RESEARCH
JEAN-CLAUDE LAMONTAGNE
SYNDICAT DE L'AIL ROSE DE LAUTREC

ROSIE FORD FOR ADDITIONAL HELP

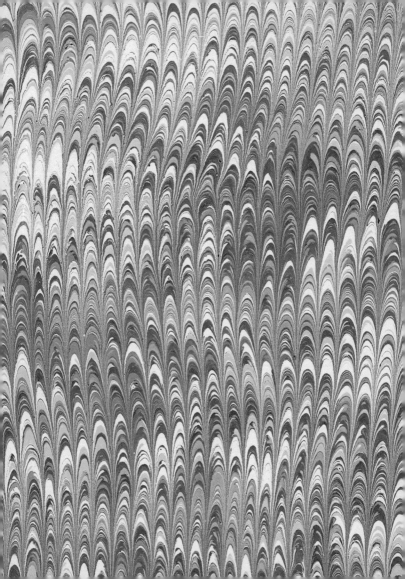